The Beatles made their American TV debut on "The Ed Sullivan Show" in February 1964.

𝕮𝖔𝖗𝖓𝖊𝖗𝖘𝖙𝖔𝖓𝖊𝖘 𝖔𝖋 𝕱𝖗𝖊𝖊𝖉𝖔𝖒

The Story of
TELEVISION

By Zachary Kent

CHILDRENS PRESS®
CHICAGO

NBC's television broadcast from the New York World's Fair in 1939

Library of Congress Cataloging-in-Publication Data

Kent, Zachary.

   The story of television / by Zachary Kent.
     p.   cm. — (Cornerstones of freedom)
   Summary: Discusses how television began as an
entertainment form and grew to be also an instrument to
teach, illuminate, and inspire.
   ISBN 0-516-04749-3
   1. Television—United States—History—Juvenile
literature. [1. Television—History.] I. Title.
II. Series.
PN1992.57.K45 1990   89-48667
791.45'0973—dc20   CIP
                                          AC

Thousands of Americans gathered on the land-scaped grounds of Flushing Meadow Park, Long Island, on April 30, 1939, to watch the formal opening of the New York World's Fair. They pressed close to the speakers' platform and listened as President Franklin D. Roosevelt dedicated the fair. Some people in the crowd noticed a strange-looking camera recording the ceremony. The camera was owned by the National Broadcasting Company (NBC), a division of Radio Corporation of America (RCA). A cable connected the camera to a van near-by. Equipment inside the van sent pictures to two hundred television sets scattered in homes around the New York City area. Some two thousand people gazed with delight as Roosevelt became the first American president ever to appear on television.

Afterward, outside the RCA pavilion, curious visitors watched as a television camera recorded the

The 1939 New York World's Fair celebrated advances in science and the arts.

5

visual image and the spoken words of RCA president David Sarnoff. That very day, Sarnoff boldly announced, RCA was launching "a new industry, based on imagination, on scientific research and accomplishment . . . a new art so important . . . that it is bound to affect all society. . . ." Sarnoff promised the start of the first regular schedule of television broadcasting in the United States.

Inside the pavilion, hundreds of visitors crowded around RCA's television exhibits. The display included TV sets with 5-inch and 9-inch picture tubes costing from $200 to $675. "The first set,"

A black-and-white TV on display in the RCA pavilion at the New York World's Fair.

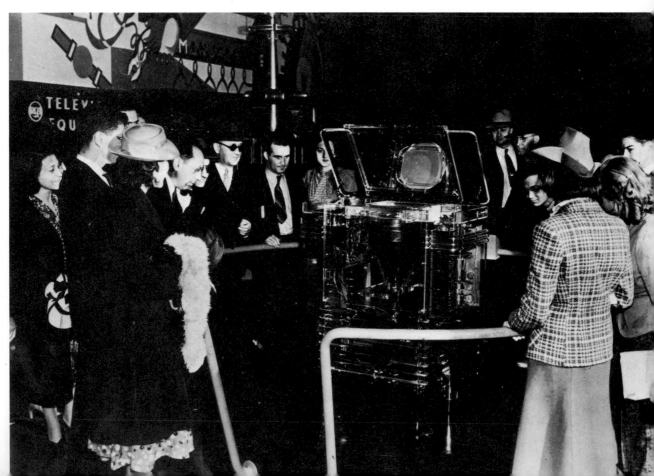

NBC producer Burke Crotty later recalled, "was called the TRK 660. It was a huge thing, stood possibly . . . 4½ feet high. It had a hinged lid with a mirror inside, and you lifted the lid and looked at the picture reflected in the mirror. . . ."

Brilliant research teams had spent years making television possible. In the months that followed Sarnoff's announcement, the NBC television studio at Radio City in New York provided eight to twelve hours of broadcasts each week. The miracle of television thrilled those Americans who watched it, but strangely, TV sets failed to sell. Another ten years of development would be required before television became a part of most American homes.

People first dared to dream of television in the 1870s. With the inventions of the telephone by Alexander Graham Bell in 1876 and the phonograph by Thomas Alva Edison in 1877, people were able to transmit words. Scientists next experimented in adding sight to sound. German inventor Paul Nipkow made the Nipkow disk in 1884. Small holes punched in the disk formed a spiral pattern. As the disk turned, a shining beam created dots of light that performed a rapid scanning movement and sent pictures a short distance. With mechanical scanning methods such as this, scientists hoped one day to transmit pictures by wire.

In the 1890s, the development of motion-picture cameras by various inventors, including Edison, sparked the exciting new movie industry. The invention of wireless radio in 1895 changed the world, too. Italian inventor Guglielmo Marconi's amazing device allowed sound to speed electronically through the air on radio waves for great distances. By the 1920s, hundreds of commercial radio stations offered regular broadcasts.

Throughout these years, scientists kept experimenting with television. In 1925, British inventor John L. Baird demonstrated a crude rotating disk transmitter at a London department store. Amazed shoppers stared at the flickering images of people and objects on a tiny screen. That same year,

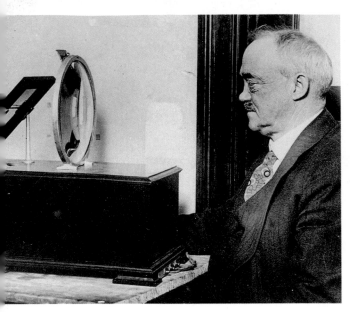

Charles F. Jenkins with an early TV set designed for home use (left). Ernst F. W. Alexanderson projected TV onto a screen for the first time in 1927 (right).

American inventor Charles F. Jenkins displayed his mechanical system for "radio vision" as he called it. On a 6- by 8-inch screen, Jenkins transmitted the blurred silhouette of a windmill turning in the wind.

In 1926, Ernst F. W. Alexanderson, who headed a research team at General Electric Company in Schenectady, New York, used spinning disks to project images onto a pink-tinged screen. Also, the American Telephone and Telegraph Company (AT&T) spent millions trying to develop mechanical television. In 1927, AT&T scientists transmitted the live image of then Secretary of Commerce Herbert Hoover across a distance of 200 miles. "LIKE A PHOTO COME TO LIFE . . . TELEVISION TRIUMPHS," proclaimed *The New York Times*.

Some scientists rejected the idea of mechanical television. They believed a television system using only electronic parts would work better. In 1923, Vladimir Zworykin, a Russian immigrant working at the Westinghouse Electric Company, invented a cathode-ray scanning tube. Called an iconoscope, the tube's fluorescent screen lit up with crude television images when bombarded by electrons. Soon RCA hired Zworykin. RCA wanted Zworykin to continue his research on this amazing electronic eye.

Another young scientist made equally thrilling advances in electronic television. As a boy on an Idaho farm, Philo T. Farnsworth pored over science magazines and dreamed about electronic television. One day, as the fourteen-year-old was plowing a sugar-beet field, he gazed back to see if the furrowed rows were straight, and a brilliant thought suddenly struck him. Television pictures could be viewed by using dots, the impulses of electrons, to scan rapidly back and forth across lines, just like reading a page.

At sixteen, the young genius outlined his theory for the "image dissector" on a high school blackboard for one of his science teachers. The surprised teacher hardly understood the complex design, but he encouraged Farnsworth's efforts. After studying electronics at college, Farnsworth

Vladimir Zworykin with a cathode-ray tube (left). Philo T. Farnsworth demonstrates a combination picture and sound TV receiver in 1935 (right).

found some investors in California who agreed to support his television research. Farnsworth and his wife, Elma, blew glass vacuum tubes and fashioned electric circuits and camera lenses in their San Francisco apartment. Often the Farnsworths kept the blinds down in order to experiment with light. One day, several suspicious police officers knocked at the door and Farnsworth gladly showed them around. "Joe, it's all right," one officer soon called to his partner outside. "They're doing some kooky things called visions. . . ."

Finally on September 7, 1927, Farnsworth completed his breakthrough image dissector. "Well, there you have television," he simply stated. Some of his investors came to see for themselves. "When are we going to see some dollars in this thing, Farnsworth?" one of the investors complained. The smiling twenty-one-year-old inventor immediately transmitted the clear image of a dollar sign through the tube. Within months, Farnsworth switched to film. On his television, he repeatedly showed segments of a Jack Dempsey-Gene Tunney prizefight and a scene of actress Mary Pickford combing her hair. In time, David Sarnoff, president of RCA, negotiated a contract that allowed RCA to use Farnsworth's various patents. By combining the best features of Zworykin's iconoscope and Farnsworth's image dissector, commercial electronic television became a real possibility at last.

RCA pushed research at its Camden, New Jersey, laboratory. Philco, Zenith, and other American companies also spent research money on television. Working independently, Edwin H. Armstrong in 1933 invented a new radio system called frequency modulation or FM. FM enabled excited RCA engineers to produce television pictures with sound. In 1935, carpenters built a studio at Radio City in New York City's Rockefeller Center. In Studio 3H, NBC began producing experimental television programs.

David Sarnoff (above) announced at the New York World's Fair that home viewers would be receiving TV programs transmitted by the Farnsworth television system (bottom left).

On July 7, 1936, NBC aired its first program, a variety show, for a few hundred viewers. By the spring of 1939, RCA president Sarnoff was ready to launch regular television service. Few people rushed out to buy RCA television sets, however. NBC producer Burke Crotty understood why. "I bought a brand-new car in 1940 for a thousand dollars," he explained, "and they wanted $660 for this TV set when there was virtually nothing on the air. At that price . . . no one wanted them." One radio magazine called television "Sarnoff's Folly."

The first TV baseball broadcast showed Columbia playing Princeton in New York in 1939.

NBC showed baseball games, old cartoons, and movies but schedules usually offered less than fifteen hours of shows a week. Technical standards remained poor, too. Performers sweated under intense lighting in those early days, and actors laughed as makeup artists colored their faces with purple lipstick and green shadows to obtain a "natural" look on camera.

As the United States plunged into World War II in December 1941, only about 10,000 American families owned television sets. The war halted further production, but progress in broadcasting continued. At RCA, for example, physicist Vladimir Zworykin invented the image-orthicon, a sensitive camera tube that allowed more comfortable studio lighting conditions. By war's end in 1945, black-and-white television had become much more practical. Returning from war service, General David Sarnoff told RCA executives, "Gentlemen, the RCA has one priority: television...This time we're going to get the job done. There's a vast market out there...." Cheaper sets with better picture quality soon

Television became more affordable with the introduction of low-cost sets. This television set sold for $100.

Workers making TV sets on an assembly line in 1947 (left). A seven-foot color wheel was needed for a mechanical color television system (right).

attracted buyers. During the next three years, TV salesmen sold more than 170,000 new models.

Four major television networks were in operation in 1948: NBC, the Columbia Broadcasting System (CBS), the American Broadcasting Companies (ABC), and DuMont. ABC had been formed in 1943 when NBC sold one of its two radio networks. DuMont, the weakest television network, created by television inventor Allen B. DuMont, struggled along until 1955. Wrestling matches and other sporting events filled much of the networks' early broadcasting schedules. Many local tavern owners installed TV sets to attract sports fans.

16

Then in 1948 NBC launched the "Texaco Star Theater," television's first smash hit. This Tuesday-night variety show starred comedian Milton Berle, whose broad humor and funny costumes attracted millions of viewers. In Ohio, one manager put a sign on his theater door: "CLOSED TUESDAY—I WANT TO SEE BERLE, TOO!" To compete with NBC, CBS quickly developed its own show. Hosted by newspaper columnist Ed Sullivan, "Toast of the Town" became a big hit too. For the next twenty-three years, viewers tuned in every Sunday night to see Sullivan introduce his many guests.

Milton Berle with Ethel Merman on the "Texaco Star Theater" (left). Sammy Davis, Jr., visits "The Ed Sullivan Show" (right).

Sid Caesar and Imogene Coca (left). Fran Allison and puppeteer Burr Tillstrom with puppets Kukla and Ollie the dragon (center). Host Bob Smith with Howdy Doody and Zippy the chimp (right).

Soon other programs boosted television sales. "Your Show of Shows" starring comedian Sid Caesar was a hit on Saturday nights. Crime shows like "Mr. District Attorney" and "Man Against Crime" also excited television watchers. Children enjoyed the puppets on "Howdy Doody" and "Kukla, Fran and Ollie." A number of radio stars such as Jack Benny, Bob Hope, and George Burns and Gracie Allen successfully developed television programs.

NBC's nightly fifteen-minute "Camel News Caravan," sponsored by Camel Cigarettes and hosted by John Cameron Swayze, became television's first regular news show in 1947. Respected reporter Edward R. Murrow sometimes changed public opinion with his documentary news series "See It Now." NBC's early morning "Today" show combined news with variety when it started in 1952. Its popularity skyrocketed after a cute chimpanzee named J. Fred Muggs joined host Dave Garroway on the show.

The early years of television earned the nickname "The Golden Age" mostly because of its original

Early TV news programs featured John Cameron Swayze (left), Edward R. Murrow (center), and Dave Garroway, shown at right with J. Fred Muggs.

Comedian Jackie Gleason with Betsy Palmer in a dramatic role on "Playhouse 90" (left). William Frawley, Vivian Vance, and Desi Arnaz (left to right) with Lucille Ball and canine friend on "I Love Lucy."

dramas. On "Studio One," "The U.S. Steel Hour," "Kraft Television Theater," and "Playhouse 90," many playwrights were featured. Teleplays like "Marty" by Paddy Chayefsky and "Requiem for a Heavyweight" by Rod Serling, who later created "The Twilight Zone," portrayed deeply human situations. Performing on live television frightened many actors. Anything could happen. "There were always disasters," remembered lighting director Imero Fiorentino. "There were many shows where

scenery fell down; it just fell down on camera
...There was nothing you could do about it."

The Golden Age of live television came to an end as television programs switched to film. If actors made mistakes while filming a show, they just reshot the scene. Afterward, a film editor put the best scenes together to create the finished show. "I Love Lucy" starring Lucille Ball and Desi Arnaz, became America's first filmed TV show in 1951. Soon another series filmed in Hollywood challenged "I Love Lucy" as TV's leading show. "Just the facts, ma'am," requested Jack Webb playing the part of Sergeant Joe Friday on "Dragnet." The first police series, "Dragnet" included outdoor action scenes and car chases. In time, most networks closed their live television studios in New York and headed for the film studios of Hollywood.

By 1952, TV was an important American institution. Sponsors noticed that sales of their products, ranging from toothpaste to automobiles, zoomed upward after advertising on television. Business at restaurants and nightclubs dropped as people stayed home to watch TV. Book sales and record sales slumped, and a sudden drop in attendance closed many movie theaters across the country.

In 1955, the Hollywood motion-picture studios also started producing TV shows in order to survive.

Western fans watched Clayton Moore as the Lone Ranger and Jay Silverheels as his Indian companion Tonto (left), Hugh O'Brien as Wyatt Earp (center), and Fess Parker in coonskin cap as Davy Crockett (right).

Warner Brothers made the first series, a Western called "Cheyenne." "Cheyenne" proved so popular that it started a Western craze. Soon other Westerns such as "Maverick," "Wyatt Earp," "Wagon Train," and "Gunsmoke" filled network schedules. Walt Disney Studios started another national fad when it aired "The Adventures of Davy Crockett" starring Fess Parker. Children everywhere wore buckskin shirts and raccoon hats.

In the 1950s family-oriented comedy shows such as "Father Knows Best," "Ozzie and Harriet," and "Leave It to Beaver" were popular. Crime shows such as "Racket Squad," "Highway Patrol," and

Jane Wyatt, Robert Young, and TV family in "Father Knows Best" (left). A delighted contestant wins a big cash prize on "Treasure Hunt" (right).

"Perry Mason" soon attracted wide audiences. Americans also hurried home to watch musical variety shows hosted by Liberace, Lawrence Welk, and Perry Como.

Large cash prizes and amazing information got people watching game shows. "The $64,000 Question" became the first big success in 1955, followed by others like "Treasure Hunt," "I've Got a Secret," "Beat the Clock," and "Concentration." In 1959, a major scandal erupted when a contestant on a quiz show admitted he had been given answers in advance. His testimony cast a dark shadow on the honesty of quiz shows for a time.

The first color TV was manufactured in 1954 (left). In the 1955 color telecast of "Peter Pan" (right), Mary Martin repeated for the television audience the part she had played on the Broadway stage.

As early as 1940, inventor Peter Goldmark of CBS had introduced a mechanical method for color television. RCA engineers, however, rejected Goldmark's "color wheel" as impractical. They worked round the clock to develop an electronic color system unveiled in July 1951. "No one could ask for better color," insisted a *Broadcasting Magazine* reporter after seeing RCA's high-definition tricolor tube. When someone asked Bob Hope how the color system worked, he joked, "[RCA president] General Sarnoff stands behind the set with color crayons."

RCA began selling its bulky, expensive color sets

The young Mousketeers of "The Mickey Mouse Club" (left). The Cartwright family of "Bonanza" (center). Robert Stack as G-man Eliot Ness battled gangsters on "The Untouchables" (right).

in 1954. A 1955 color broadcast of "Peter Pan" starring Mary Martin excited many viewers. By 1960, color TV really caught on when Walt Disney introduced "Walt Disney's Wonderful World of Color." A new Western series called "Bonanza" was also filmed in vivid color. "Bonanza" soon rose to number one in the TV ratings.

"The Untouchables" in 1959, and shows like "77 Sunset Strip," "Hawaiian Eye," and "The Rifleman" followed quickly. Teenagers stayed glued to their television sets for up to five hours a day. Some teachers and parents argued that so much television

Bill Cosby and Robert Culp in "I Spy" (left). A bereaved nation watched as President John F. Kennedy was laid to rest in Arlington National Cemetery (right).

viewing was unhealthy. Newton Minow, chairman of the Federal Communications Commission, warned: "When television is bad, nothing is worse . . . you will see . . . blood and thunder, mayhem, violence . . . murder . . . private eyes, gangsters, more violence, and cartoons. And endlessly, commercials — many screaming, cajoling, and offending. . . ."

Television offered all kinds of entertainment in the 1960s. Dramatic doctor shows such as "Dr. Kildare" and "Ben Casey" were popular. "Peyton Place" became the first nighttime soap opera in 1964. In the action show "I Spy" in 1965 Bill Cosby became the first black actor to appear in a starring role on a dramatic series. Comedies like "The Beverly Hillbillies," "The Munsters," and the skits on "Laugh-In" caught the wild spirit of the late 1960s.

Television covered worldwide news events. With dinner trays balanced on their laps, Americans watched nightly news reports given by Chet Huntley and David Brinkley on NBC and Walter Cronkite on CBS. Politicians increasingly used television to promote their campaigns. Massachusetts Senator John F. Kennedy used television during his 1960 race for the White House. After he won the close election, Kennedy said, "We wouldn't have had a prayer without that gadget."

In July 1962, a communications satellite called *Telstar I* was sent into orbit around the earth. *Telstar* thrust television into the space age, allowing live events to be transmitted by satellite relay around the globe. Sadly, the assassination of President Kennedy on Friday, November 22, 1963, in Dallas, Texas, became one news story that soon made television history. More than 700 million tearful people worldwide watched the funeral procession that accompanied Kennedy's coffin to Washington's Arlington National Cemetery.

Through the 1960s, television covered the civil rights movement in the United States and the war in

Millions of earthbound viewers saw the astronauts land on the moon (left).
The Bunker family of "All in the Family" (center). Le Var Burton played Kunta Kinte
in the phenomenal miniseries "Roots" (right).

Vietnam. Live coverage of the *Apollo XI* mission on July 20, 1969, stirred the hearts and minds of 720 million viewers worldwide.

As television entered the 1970s, programmers increasingly found ways to comment on society. The successful series "M*A*S*H" first aired in 1972. The hilarious sitcom "All in the Family" dealt with real-life social issues from 1971 to 1983.

The Watergate cover-up became the great news story of the 1970s. Testimony about illegal activities in the White House kept television viewers outraged and fascinated day after day. Finally they watched President Richard Nixon appear on television on August 9, 1974, and resign from office.

A new TV concept called the miniseries developed in the late 1970s. Over several nights, a network showed episodes of a continuing drama. The first miniseries, "Roots," premiered on ABC in 1977. Millions of Americans nightly followed the progress of the slave Kunta Kinte and his family. "More people saw 'Roots' in that one week," marveled television producer David Wolper afterward, "than have seen Shakespeare in all the performances on stage since he wrote the plays."

As television programming raced through the 1980s it seemed some shows would last forever. Teenagers had been dancing on ABC's "American Bandstand," hosted by Dick Clark, since 1957. Hosting the long-running "Tonight" show on NBC since 1962, Johnny Carson still kept late-night viewers laughing. Since 1968, the CBS news series "60 Minutes" had been exploring current events and profiling interesting people every Sunday evening.

Dick Clark and teenage fans on "American Bandstand" in 1958.

"The Cosby Show" was the most popular sitcom of the mid-1980s (left). Philip
Michael Thomas and Don Johnson starred in the detective series "Miami Vice"
(center). Vanna White and Pat Sajak, hosts of the successful game show "Wheel of
Fortune" (right).

Television in the 1980s also offered wider viewing
choices than ever before. Nonprofit public television
stations are largely supported by viewer contribu-
tions and are served by the Public Broadcasting
Service (PBS). PBS has provided the wonderful
learning show "Sesame Street" for children since
1969. Other PBS programming includes operas,
classic films, and documentaries. The arrival of
cable television in the 1980s allowed paying
customers to see movies on HBO, music videos on
MTV, sports on ESPN, and news on CNN.

The 1980s Japanese invention of the videocassette recorder (VCR) enabled people to tape programs and watch movies on their televisions. Today, Americans take home more videocassettes than library books.

Today, more than 2.5 billion people regularly watch television on 750 million sets in more than 160 countries. Every day, 250,000 new TV sets roll off production lines. Critics of television call it the "boob tube" and the "idiot box." Yet television remains a truly remarkable invention. It has made the world smaller and its people closer. Through television we have shared the tragedy of the *Challenger* space shuttle disaster, and watched political change in the U.S.S.R., China, and Eastern Europe. Long ago, newsman Edward R. Murrow correctly realized, "This instrument can teach, it can illuminate; yes, it can even inspire." Since 1939, television has spread knowledge like no other invention, and through its eye we surely gain a greater understanding of life.

Harry Reasoner, Ed Bradley, Diane Sawyer, Morley Safer (standing, left to right), and Mike Wallace (seated) appeared on the long-running news series "60 Minutes."

INDEX

About the Author

Zachary Kent grew up in Little Falls, New Jersey, and received an English degree from St. Lawrence University. Following college he worked at a New York City literary agency for two years and then launched his writing career. To support himself while writing, he has worked as a taxi driver, a shipping clerk, and a house painter. Mr. Kent has had a lifelong interest in American history.